EMOTIMANIA

Do you love all things emoti?
Then this activity book is perfect for you!
Inside you will find:

Fun activity pages, cool emoti puffy
stickers, and cute, emoti press-outs
to display or give away!

How to use your press-out pieces:

BRILLIANT BOOKMARKS

Press out and decorate the bookmarks.

1 Pull out the card pages at
the back of the book.

2 Gently push the shapes
until they pop out.

3 Complete the press-out
pieces using doodles, color,
and your puffy stickers.

make believe ideas

EMOTI DICTIONARY

Use color to finish the emotis.

 angelic

 bear

 best friends

 birthday

 bow

 bowling

 bunny

 butterfly

 cactus

 camera

 celebration

 chick

 cool

 crown

 cycling

 dancing

 days out

 diamond

 dizzy

 dolphin

 eating

 elephant

 excited

 family

 fish

 flamingo

 flattered

 flower

 friends

 frog

 games

 gaming

 geeky

 good

 grandma

 grandpa

 guitar

 hair flick

 happy

 heart

 kisses

 koala

 ladybug

 lightning

 lion

 lipstick

 love

 makeup

Circle the emotis you like best.

 mermaid

 moon

 mouse

 music

 nail polish

 no deal

 octopus

 overjoyed

 painting

 painting nails

 panda

 party time

 pig

playing music

princess

 pug

 puppy

 question

 rainbow

 raining

 reading

 robot

 rose

 sad

 scared

 secret

 shocked

 shoe shopping

 silly

 singing

 sleepy

 snake

 snowing

 special occasion

 sports

star

 storm

 strong

 sunglasses

 sunny

 television

 tennis

 thank you

 tiger

 traveling

 turtle

 umbrella

 unicorn

 whale

3

MY FRIENDS

In the frames, draw your friends as emotis.

Best friend

Océane

Write your friend's name here.

Jillian

Blessing

Gabriellerie

Paige W. (my famly.)

Ella

Sofia

Jessie

MERMAID MAZE

Use the key to help the mermaid through the maze.

Start

Finish

SUMMER FUN

Find all eight emotis in the grid.
Words can go across, down, or diagonally.

butterfly ✓

dress

flowers

```
p i n e a p p l e s | s
s u n v b t d r e a | a
f r d e s h e l l | n
l g e r e a t b a | d
o w c s e l s e r a | a
w u e r s s s l k | l
e c a l o m s t c | s
r b u t t e r f l y
s u n g l a s s e s
```

pineapple ✓

sandals ✓

shell ✓

sun ✓

sunglasses ✓

Decorate the butterflies
and color the flowers.

EMOTI NAILS

Design amazing emoti nail art.

Doodle some more emoti bracelets and rings.

PUTTING ON A SHOW

Can you help the singer find her lost microphone?

Start →

Finish

Finish the audience emotis:

EMOTI HAPPY

Design your own emotis for the
things that make you smile!

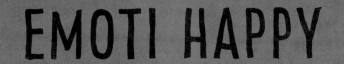
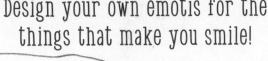

 food
PEOPLE

ice-cream

candy

People
FOOD

Océane

Jillian

11

EMOTI-SHIRT

Draw and doodle cool emoti designs on the T-shirts.

CUTE CUPCAKES

Color and decorate the emoti cupcakes.

MONKEY MADNESS

Which monkey is the one that doesn't fit?

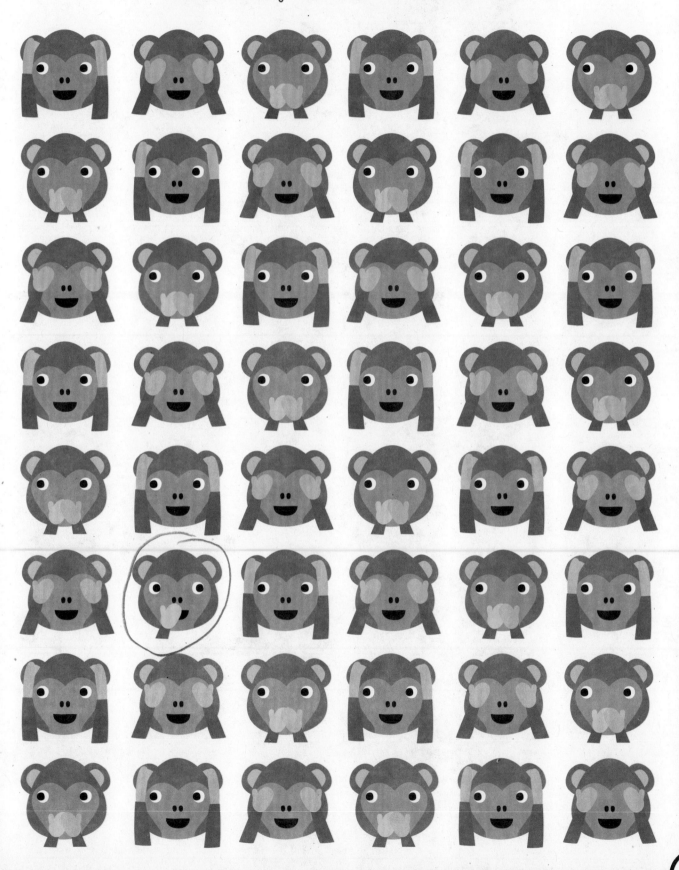

WHICH EMOTI ARE YOU?

START

Choose which emoti you like best and follow the arrows until you reach the end of the quiz. Then check the emoti you are most like!

SWEET COOKIE

Your friends and family love you because you are so sweet and thoughtful.

PARTY SHOE

You are the life and soul of any party and love dancing and having fun.

CUTE PUPPY

You love animals and are very good at cheering people up when they are feeling upset.

DOODLE TIME

Doodle emoti faces in the yellow circles.

EMOTI ART

Copy the emotis. Use the grids to help you.

MY FAMILY

In the frames, draw members of your family as emotis.

Paige

Write each person's name here.

Nicole

MoM

DaD

Nicole

Steve

Josh

Josh

21

WHAT'S IN MY BAG?

Doodle three emotis for the things you
would need if you were going to . . .

A SLEEPOVER

SCHOOL

THE BEACH

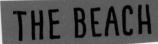

COMPLETE THE CIRCLE

Fill the circle with more emoti faces.

Try to include
these emotis:

MY EMOTI SLEEPOVER

Design emoti pajamas for you and your friends
to wear at your emoti sleepover!

Color the sleepover activities, and then circle your top three.

Color the midnight snacks, and then circle your top three.

Doodle emotis on your overnight bag.

WINTER WISHES

Find all eight emotis in the grid.
Words can go across, down, or diagonally.

coat ✓

hat ✓

igloo ✓

mittens ✓

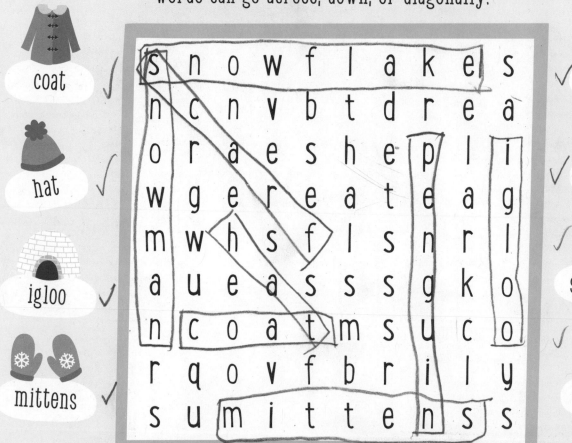

penguin ✓

scarf ✓

snowflake ✓

snowman ✓

s	n	o	w	f	l	a	k	e	s
n	c	n	v	b	t	d	r	e	a
o	r	a	e	s	h	e	p	l	i
w	g	e	r	e	a	t	e	a	g
m	w	h	s	f	l	s	n	r	l
a	u	e	a	s	s	g	r	k	o
n	c	o	a	t	m	s	u	c	o
r	q	o	v	f	b	r	i	l	y
s	u	m	i	t	t	e	n	s	s

Finish the scarf, hat, and mittens with emoti designs.

Rearrange the letters to
make a winter word.

RSAFC

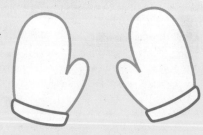

26

DANCING QUEEN

Use the key to help the dancer
through the maze!

Start

Finish

1ST

EMOTI PAIRS

Draw lines to join the pairs of emotis. Can you join them without any of your lines crossing each other?

MAGICAL UNICORNS

Complete the unicorns using rainbow colors.

EMOTI FUN

Design your own emotis for the things you think are really fun!

ACTIVITIES

Arts

Singin

PLACES

Camping

going to see Brianna

KITTEN CRAZY

Which kitten is the one that doesn't fit?

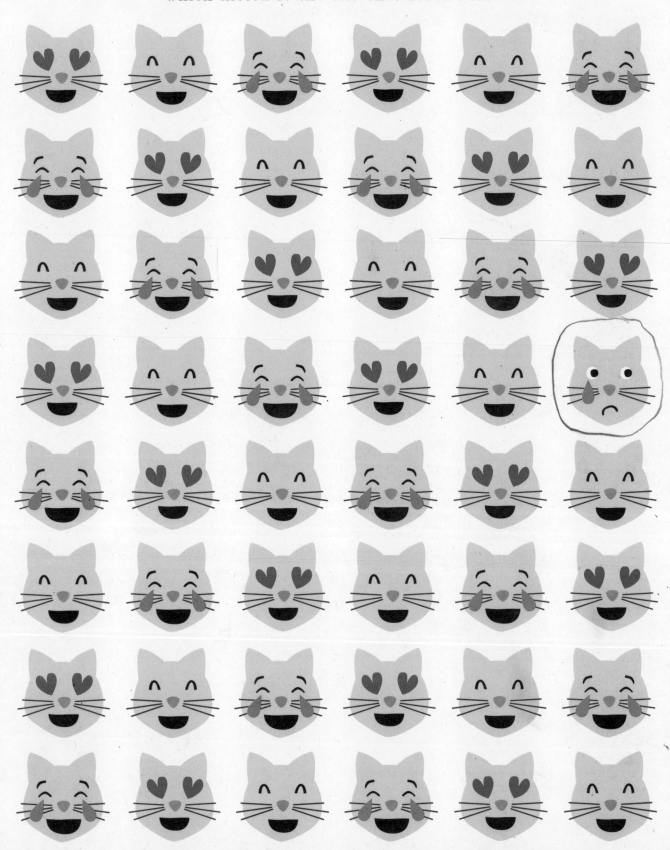

PALACE PARTY

Can you help the princess find
her special party crown?

Start

Finish

Finish the
party emotis:

EMOTI STYLE

Create emoti designs for the
beautiful bags, shoes, and dresses.

Color and finish the beautiful flower garden.

Rearrange the letters to make garden words.

RFLWOE   TCAUSC

Color and finish the flower emotis. Use the grids to help you.

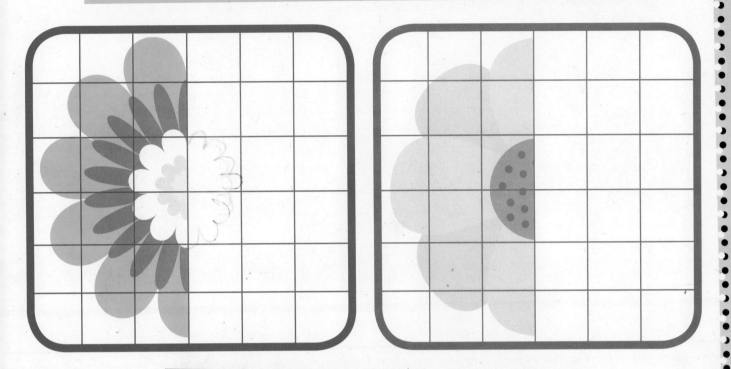

Finish the weather emotis and circle the top two that will help your garden grow.

Doodle emoti beads and charms
to create unique necklaces.

EMOTI ART

Copy the emotis. Use the grids to help you.

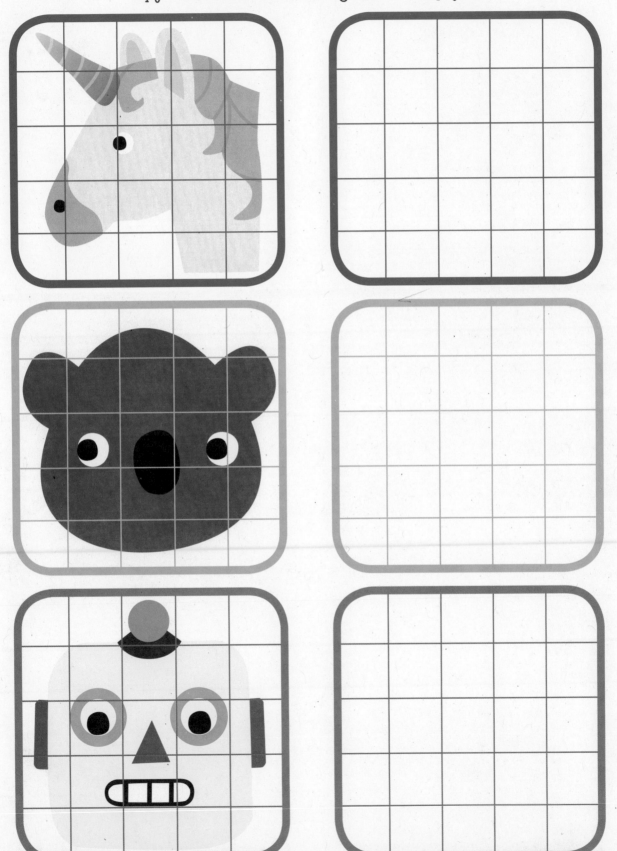

DREAM PETS

In the frames, draw emotis of your dream pets.

Give your dream pet a name.

Flubs

Sparcle

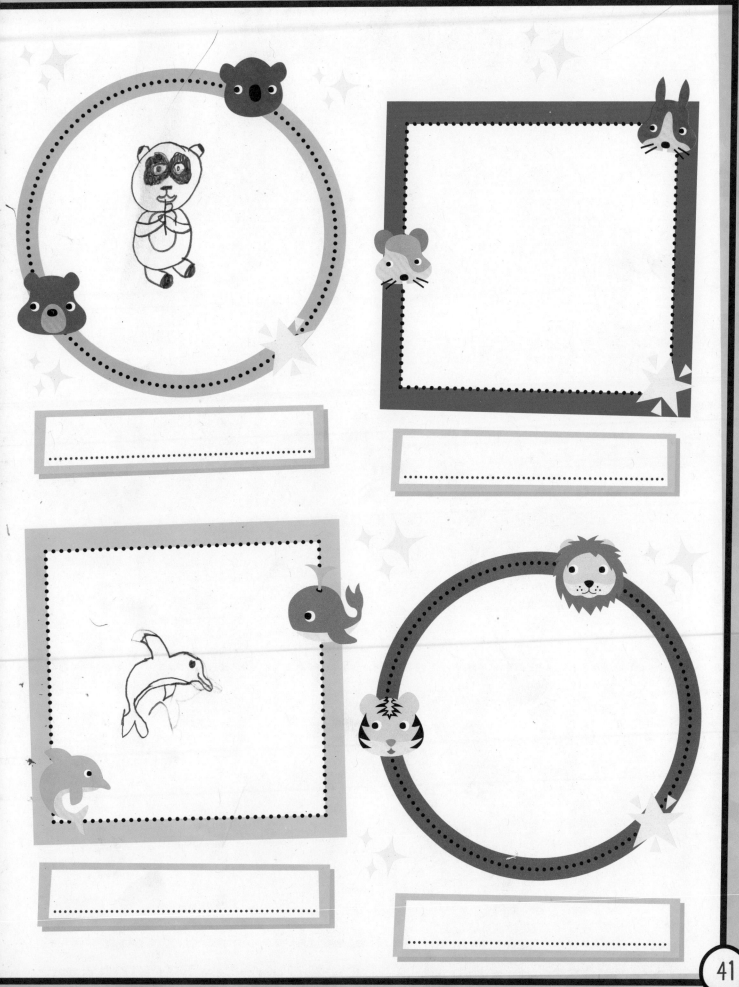

Finish coloring the yummy treats.

Draw your own emoti snacks here.

ISLAND STYLE

Find all eight emotis in the grid.
Words can go across, down, or diagonally.

bag

fish

flamingo

hat

magazine

plane

tree

watermelon

```
p h a t a p p f e s
w a t e r m e l o n
f r r e p h e a l n
l g e r e l t m o d
o w e s e l a i r a
w m a g a z i n e l
e c a l o b a g e s
r b p t t v r o l y
s f i s h a l s q s
```

Draw emotis of the three things you'd need
if you were shipwrecked on an island!

LOVE HEARTS

Fill the heart with emotis of the things you love.

FILL-IN FACES

Complete the emoti faces, giving each a unique style.

MY EMOTI DESIGNS

Design new emotis for these different things:

CAMPING

DINOSAUR

COOKING

HOMEWORK

CASTLE

SCHOOL

SELFIE

SURFING

JUNGLE GYM

Use the key to help the
monkey through the maze!

Start

Finish

TASTY TREATS

Complete the ice-cream cones using yummy colors.

FUNNY FACES

Which emoti face doesn't fit?

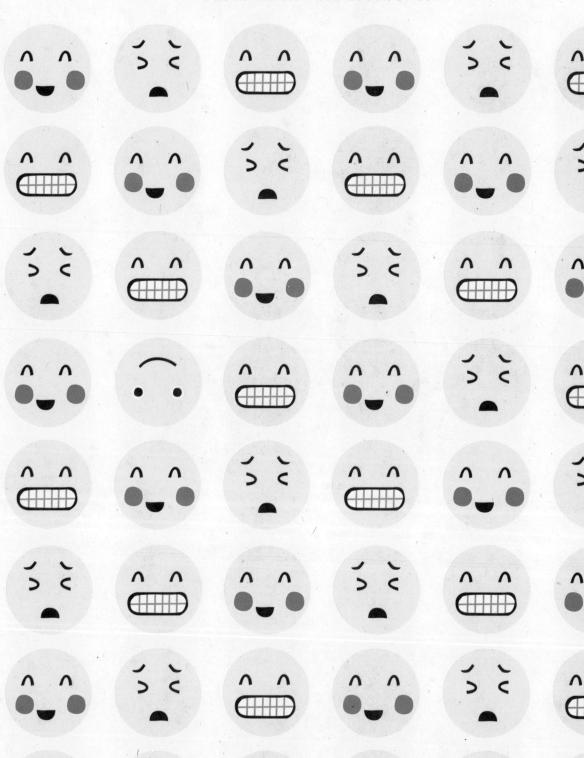

BEAUTIFUL BUTTERFLIES

Complete the butterfly scene using pretty colors.

EMOTI FAVES

Design emotis for your
favorite things!

TREASURES

CLOTHES

STYLE THE SHOES

Design a pair of emoti shoes. They can both match or be completely different!

EMOTI ART

Copy the emotis. Use the grids to help you.

KEEP FIT

Can you help the athlete find her tennis racket?

Start

Finish

Finish the sporty emotis:

DREAM PHONE

Decorate your own emoti phone covers.

Write messages to your friends on the phone screens. You can add your fave emotis too.

FAVE CELEBS

In the frames, draw emotis of your favorite celebrities.

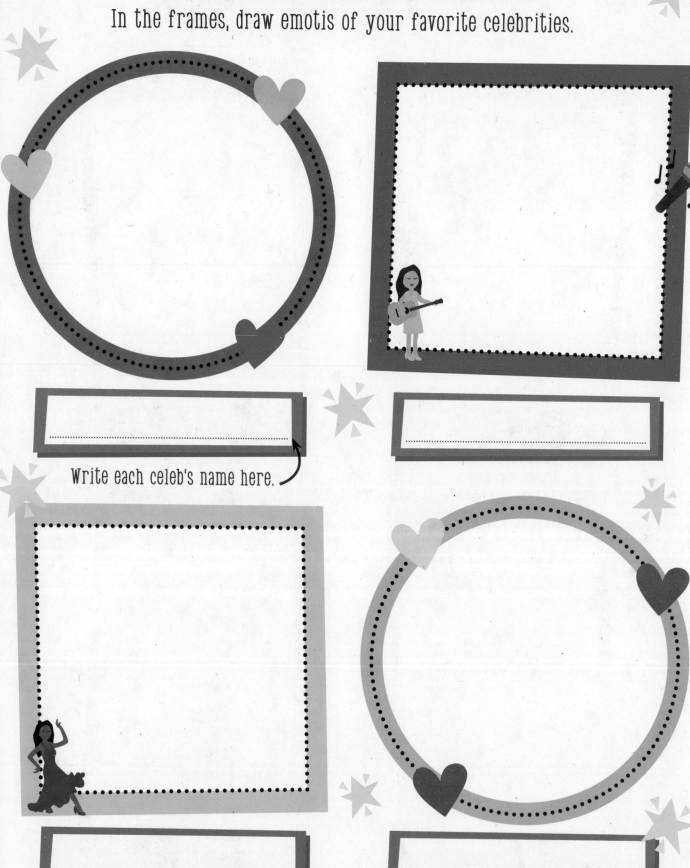

Write each celeb's name here.

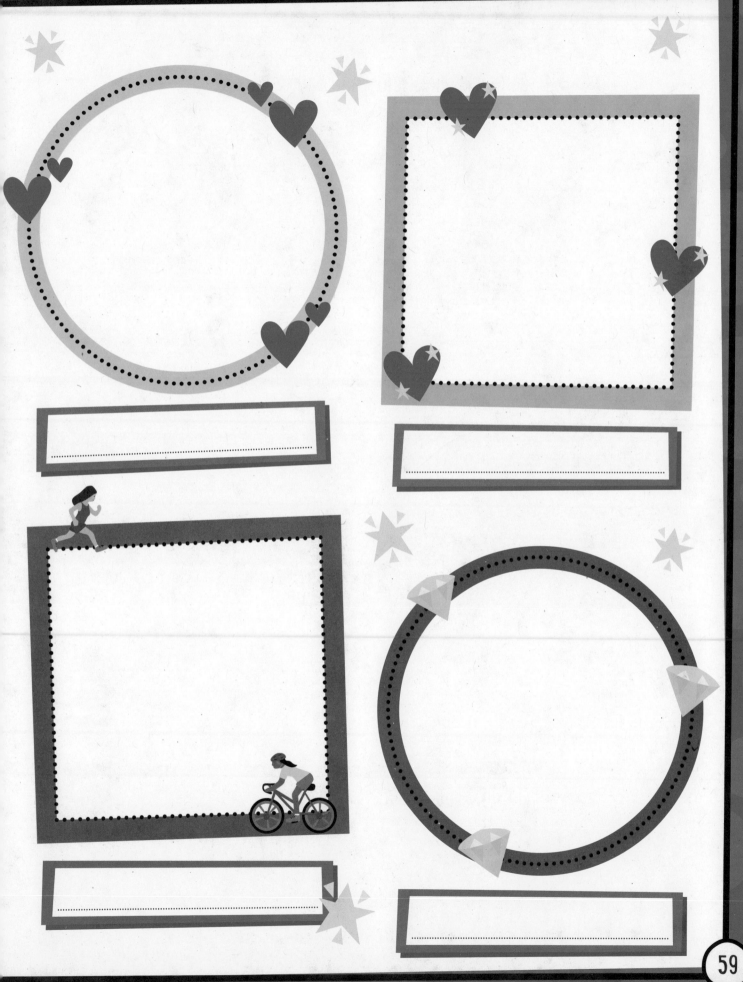

TROPICAL FISH

Complete the fish using bright colors.

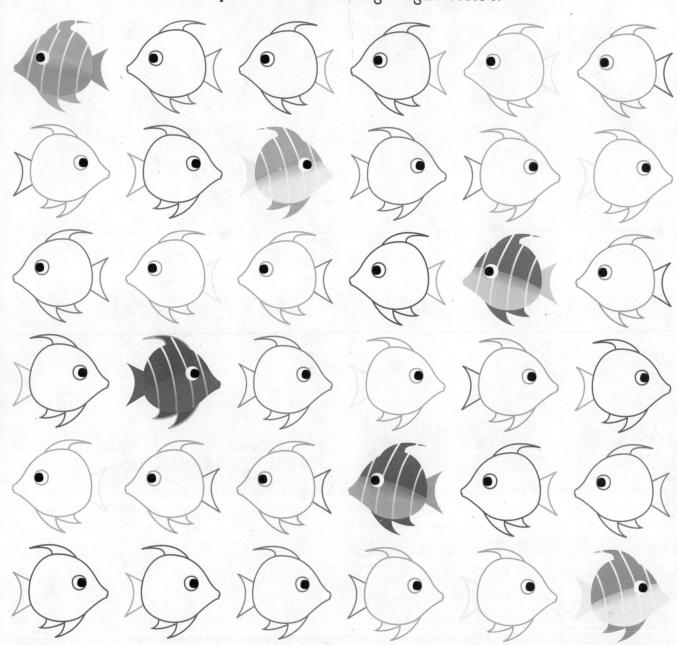

Rearrange the letters to make ocean words.

POTOUSC 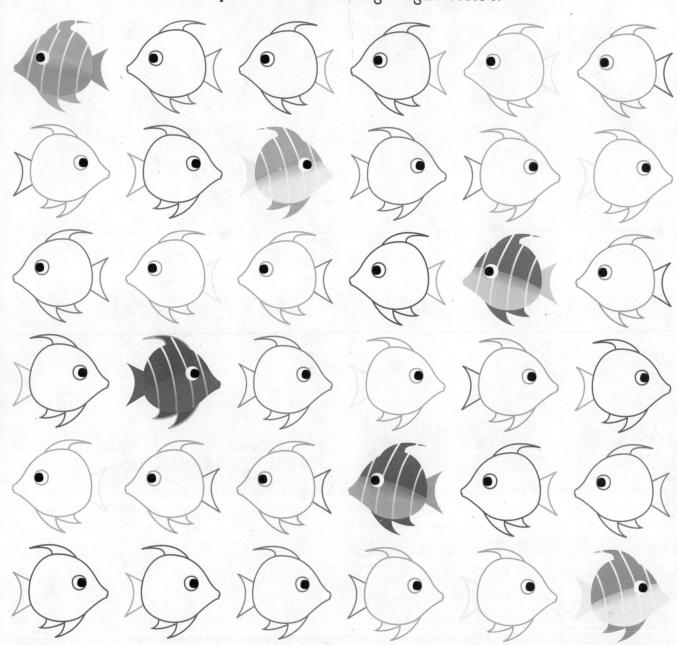   HLEWA

....

DINNERTIME

Use the key to help the hungry emoti through the maze!

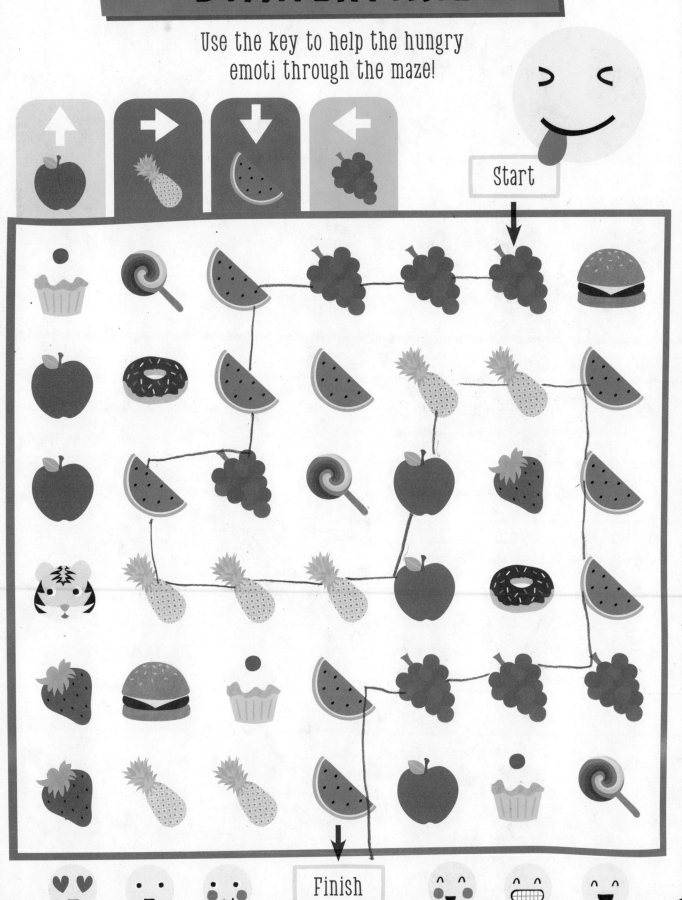

Start

Finish

FAVE EMOTIS

Look at the first page of this book and draw new versions of your four favorite emotis.

EMOTI ME

Draw yourself as your very own, unique emoti!

PERFECT PETS

Which cute animal face doesn't fit?

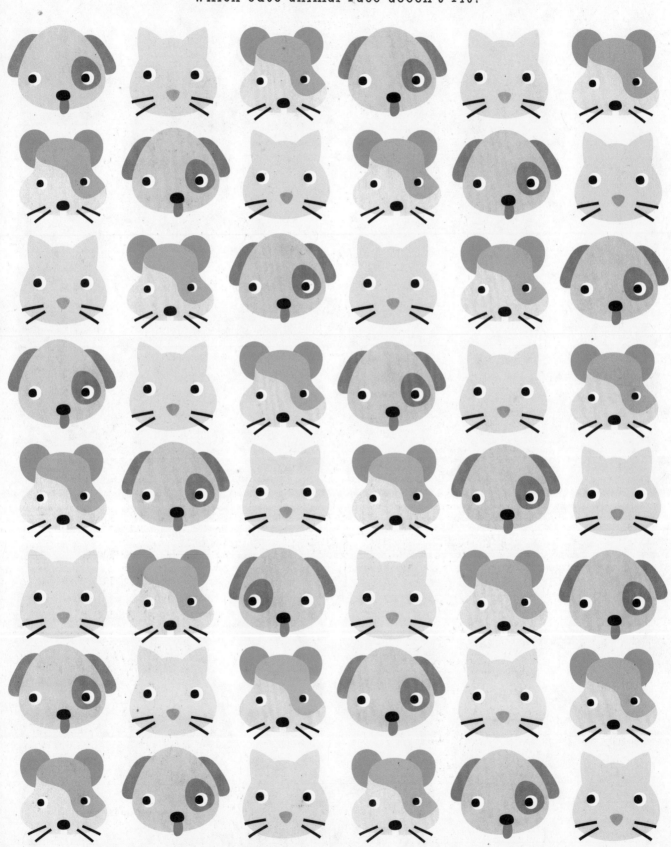

JUST TO SAY . . .

Press out and complete the card,
and then give it to a friend.

POSTCARDS

Press out and complete the postcards,
and then give them to your friends.

YOU ARE AMAZING

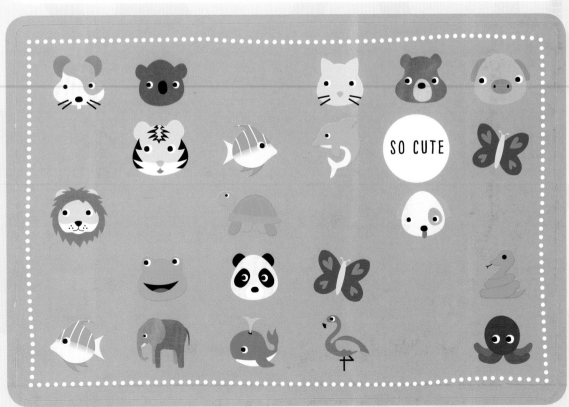

SO CUTE

BRILLIANT BOOKMARKS

Press out and decorate the bookmarks.

EMOTI FLAGS

Press out each flag and fold the tops
over some ribbon. Tape them down at the back,
and then hang them wherever you want!

JUST TO SAY . . .

Press out and complete the card,
and then give it to a friend.

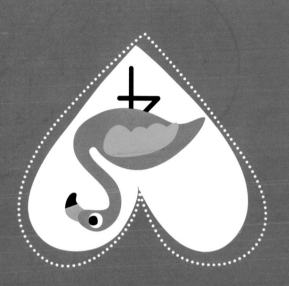

POSTCARDS

Press out and complete the postcards,
and then give them to your friends.

JUST TO SAY...